CAPTIVE THOUGHTS.....
because we are all serving time.

May these thoughts each day motivate & inspire you!

Linda O'Dell
5-5-21

Linda O'Dell - Author • Box 593 • Harrah, OK. 73045

by LINDA O'DELL

A collection of interesting thoughts, to make you think. About prison ministry and just life. To support prison ministry and to celebrate the victory Jesus brings.

1. So I spoke to those in captivity of all the things the Lord had shown me.   Ezekiel 11:25

2. Prison ministry reaches in to those reaching out for help.

3. Where light collides with darkness, Light wins! {Jesus}.

4. The Word of God, the Bible, is not bound; but accomplishes it's purpose.

5. Prison ministry brings Hope into a hopeless place.

6. What does God require of you, but to do justly, love mercy and walk humbly with your God. Micah 6:8.

7. Prison is life out of step.

8. Jesus commands us to visit prisoners, will you?

9. Life is a journey, step by step, on this road to redemption.

10. The worst prison to be in is a prison of sin.

11. Jesus has the keys to open every door.

12. Some prisons have invisible bars.

13. Jesus breaks every chain.

14. Jesus sets the captives free.

15. Incarceration is an education you don't want.

16. Real justice comes from Christ.

17. Life in a cage is not correction.

18. Christ has a purpose in your pain.

19. Hardship is the pathway to peace.

20. Jesus heals the brokenhearted and binds up their wounds. Psalm 147:3.

21. Jesus is the Key to life.

22. Restoration is to reposition someone to a useful place in society.

23. Rehabilitation restores to a good condition.

24. You can't run from yourself.

25. Forgive so your brokenness and wounds can be healed.

26. Christ has paid for our violations!

27. Christ brings freedom to life.

28. Prisoners are in captivity, but Christ frees them on the inside.

29. No matter what side of life you are on, there will be drama.

30. Prison is a wilderness experience where you learn rebellion or obedience,, your choice.

31. Wounds heal with scars, to remind you where you have been.

32. Road to redemption is a journey that begins with the first step of faith.

33. People should never be 'caged'.

34. You don't have to be in prison or addicted to need rehab. Jesus helps you recover from yourself.

35. Sometimes Christ slams the door shut to bring the help you need.

36. What doesn't kill you makes you stronger...eventually.

37. Jesus breaks the chains, stop trying to reconnect the links.

38. Mercy triumps over judgment. James 2:13.

39. Truth is a Person..Jesus Christ.

40. You can't embrace sin and Christ at the same time.

41. Failure is not forever.

42. Failure is not final.

43. Sometimes the answer to your question is no, no, no and no!

44. God allows U turns.

45. This is only temporary, it will pass.

46. What rights?

47. God exacts from you less than your iniquity deserves. Job 11:6
.

48. Who executeth judgment for the oppressed, who giveth food to the hungry, the Lord looses the prisoners. Psalm 146:7.

49. Don't flat-line without Jesus.

50. When it no longer hurts, it's over!

51. It's not about what you think it's about, but something else entirely.

52. You are stronger than you think.

53. You can choose the behavior but not the consequences.

54. Christians don't lose the capacity to sin; just the capacity to enjoy it like they once did.

55. You don't know you're in darkness, until the Light comes on.

56. Sometimes God opens a door you never knew you could walk through.

57. In life, you are either 'in' or 'out', no inbetween.

58. Those who tear their clothes in grief, will sew them back together in recovery.

59. Happiness sometimes sneaks up on you through an open door you did not see opened.

60. Love the unlovely, they need it the most.

61. Justification = just as if we never sinned.

62. There is no correction where there is no transformation by the Holy Spirit.

63. If He breaks a thing down, it cannot be rebuilt, if He imprisons a man, there can be no release. Job 12:14.

64. Imitate Christ instead of impersonating Him.

65. Focus on Christ's promises and not the yoke you need freed from.

66. Because of Christ, there is no Hell in my future.

67. We don't need 12 steps, we just need 1 Step =Jesus.

68. You are who you choose to be.

69. Delete any negative thought that tries to hold you captive.

70. Reject stinking thinking.

71. Don't believe everything you think.

72. Stop rewinding the past in your mind, record new thoughts instead.

73. Even if life implodes around you, choose peace.

74. Seek serenity

75. I will purge my hard drive of virus'.

76. If my hard drive gets a virus, I will do a major purge before any damage is done.

77. When you hit rock bottom, Christ is the Rock that you will stand on.

78. Recovery is an inside job.

79. Recovery builds and rebuilds character.

80. Think first, act second.

81. Be more concerned with your character than your appearance.

82. God uses endurance to build our character...building takes time.

83. Don't give up too easily.

84. Don't believe the lie that it will never get better.

85. You can't be who you were and who you want to be at the same time.

86. Don't judge by appearance, you can't see what's inside.

87. You didn't get into this mess instantly, it will take a process to get out.

88. Freedom leads to a happier life.

89. Jesus proclaims liberty to the captives. Isaiah 61:1.

90. On the other side of tribulation, is reward.

91. You can't change your direction overnight, but you can change your destination.

92. Life has a way of testing you by having nothing happen or having it happen all at once.

93. You can either focus on what's tearing you apart or what's holding you together.

94. Some people can break your heart by doing nothing at all.

95. Hurting someone is like throwing a rock in the ocean, not knowing how deep it will go.

96. The greatest problem with jurisprudence is to allow freedom while enforcing order.

97. Recovery is all about facing your pain, addiction is about avoiding it.

98. Do the right thing, do the next right thing, repeat.

99. Some roads you were never meant to be on.

100. When you soar with eagles, just know you will attrack hunters.

101. Be careful what you do with the best you have.

102. There's still time to change the road you're on.

103. Are you caught up in the captivity of activity?

104. Pursue what you preach.

105. What are you learning from those you are yoked to.

106. Don't allow anyone to enable you to your own demise.

107. Justice is broken.

108. This is not my home.

109. Your rules don't apply here.

110. Love someone when they least deserve it, that is when they need it the most.

111. You really can't learn from the mistakes of others, because yourself can't live their consequences.

112. Sometimes you get stuck between 'hold on' and 'turn loose'.

113. I'm responsible for what I say, not for what you understand.

114. God says lean on Him, not push.

115. Stop tripping on what's behind you.

116. Sometimes you have to get out of your own way.

117. Without love, none of the other gifts matter.

118. Stop hindering yourself.

119. You can't lead if you are not going anywhere.

120. It's not always about hitting rock bottom, but how much you bounce back when you get there.

121. We can roll the dice, but God decides where they land.

122. We are all serving time.

123. God is your 'Merriam Webster' don't let anyone else define you.

124. Jumping to conclusions is not considered exercise.

125. Feel it, deal with it, heal it.

126. Expectations are premeditated resentments.

127. If you're in a pit, stop digging!

128. To get anywhere, start where you are.

129. God is not surprised by what you say or do.

130. Mistakes happen.

131. Don't be your own victim.

132. Fear is the darkroom where negatives are developed.

133. Serenity comes when we stop expecting and start accepting.

134. Wherever you go, there you are.

135. Don't make a crisis out of an incident.

136. Hard to be hateful; when you're grateful.

137. Put Christ between you and the problem.

138. No! Is a complete sentence.

139. There's a difference being responsible to others & being responsible for others.

140. You can't reach for anything new until you let go of the old.

141. Joshua would never have learned to exercise his faith while Moses was still there.

142. The battle is the Lord's but David still had to sling that shot.

143. You can't go forward, clinging to the past.

144. Everyone is guilty of all the good that they didn't do.

145. For every brick they throw, climb higher.

146. Don't waste time trying to live someone else's life.

147. It was always Satan's plan to kill you; but Christ caught & rescued you.

148. If you're on a road you never should have been on, it's your choice to turn around or drive yourself into a ditch.

149. Some people are allergic to drugs & alcohol, they break out in handcuffs.

150. You always have a choice, choose wisely.

151. What's going on outside doesn't necessarily reflect what's going on inside.

152. Hang on there's a Son behind those clouds.

153. To be found, you must first admit you're lost.

154. Do more than just survive.

155. Remember the teacher never talks during the test, you shouldn't either.

156. Risk is trying something you're powerless over.

157. Exercise your right to address your own problems.

158. Negative circumstances can bring inaccurate thoughts.

159. Risk everything, but keep your soul intact.

160. Recovery has many positive benefits; relapse has negative ones.

161. They say you never know what you have until it's gone;
truth is you knew exactly what you had, you just never thought
you would lose it.

162. Don't tell everything you know.

163. You are defined by the walls you create yourself.

164. Trust is an expensive word.

165. Jesus helps us recover from us.

166. Sometimes pain is the only way we learn.

167. Don't make someone a priority who considers you an option.

168. See in the final analysis, it's between God & you, it was never between you and them anyway.

169. Lies have no control over you when you stop believing them.

170. Better to be hurt by truth than comforted by lies.

171. Speak truth, even if your voice shakes.

172. Let Jesus carry you, instead of trying to drag Him behind you.

173. Denial= don't even know I am lying.

174. Just for today I will rise above the chaos.

175. You don't stop one thing...you do another.

176. Just for today, I won't quit.

177. I won't deny reality, but I won't cave under it either.

178. I will try to have peace on the inside, that I appear to have on the outside.

179. If you can't control your thoughts, you won't be able to control your actions.

180. I will reject the feeling that screaming my head off will accomplish anything.

181. I will fight back & not give in to panic.

182. God grant me serenity now!

183. I will tell the voices in my head to shut up.

184. My mind is a dangerous place, I can't go there alone.

185. What feeds you, affects you.

186. Some boundaries should never be crossed.

187. Change is not change until it's changed.

188. God will never agree with the lies you tell yourself.

189. Not all wounds are visible.

190. Get over yourself.

191. Serenity rocks.

192. Our stains won't come clean without Jesus.

193. Mother's are precious but they can never be fathers.

194. Recovery begins with the first step.

195. I'm not guilty, but I am not innocent, I am justified.

196. Happiness is not getting what you want but wanting what you get.

197. It's never too late to be who you might have been.

198. You can't run someone else's race.

199. You won't change until the pain is strong enough to move you.

200. Difference between stumbling blocks & stepping stones is how you use them.

201. Glance at the past, but don't stare at it.

202. Even on the right path, you can get run over if you don't move.

203. It's not about the outside package, but the present on the inside; don't be hidden by the wrapping.

204. If you focus on the cheese, you won't see the trap.

205. The hardest journey is inward.

206. You're stronger than you think.

207. You can choose the behavior but not the consequences.

208. Life is not a smooth ride.

209. Don't let the level of your happiness affect your joy.

210. Don't base your happiness on something you could lose.

211. He who forgives, wins the argument.

212. Sometimes unspoken words are the ones that should be spoken the most.

213. God will change your attitude.

214. God doesn't call you to measure up to someone else's gift.

215. If you don't understand my silence, you don't deserve my words.

216. Taste your words before you spit them out.

217. The moment you give up is the moment you let someone else win.

218. Sometimes the very thing you're most afraid of doing is the very thing that will set you free.

219. If you can't be thankful for what you have, be thankful for what you've escaped.

220. A real friend will be there when they desire to be somewhere else.

221. Sometimes the best fragrance comes after the flower is crushed.

222. He has not dealt with us according to our sins, nor punished us according to our iniquities. Psalm 103:10.

223. Behold, I cry violence, but I get no answer. I shout for help, but there is not justice. Job 19:7.

224. If He cuts off and shuts up or gather together then who can hinder Him. Job 11:10.

225. He hath hedged me about, that I cannot get out, He hath made my chain heavy. Lamentations 3:7.

226. The heart is the center of the body but beats on the left. Maybe that is the reason the heart will never be right.

227. No one ever regrets giving.

228. Be smart enough to hang on & brave enough to let go.

229. Cracks always produce leaks, strengthen your armour.

230. Don't put the key to your happiness in someone else's pocket.

231. Character is more important than image.

232. You will never get to your destination, if you stop to throw rocks at every dog that barks.

233. When the peaceful majority remain silent they become irrelevant.

234. Love doesn't make the world go around, but it makes the ride worthwhile.

235. If you don't fight for what you want ,don't cry when you lose it.

236. If you're lying to yourself from the beginning, you can't hear anything else.

237. Stop picking up what God said to put down.

238. If you ignore the fire in the kitchen, you'll burn the whole house down.

239. Find someone who will change your life, not just your status.

240. Sometimes you got to go back to where you started from.

241. You can't find peace, avoiding life.

242. Take time to make time, this life is not forever, many things & people pass through unappreciated & absent.

243. Know what to battle or to embrace.

244. Just because you can doesn't mean you should.

245. You miss 100% of the shots you don't take.

246. Courage is the discovery that you may not win, & trying when you know you might lose.

247. Walk away or try harder?

248. Beware those who say they are on your team, but keep blocking your shots.

249. Change the things you can't accept.

250. Looking sharp is easy if you have done no work.

251. Do your thoughts go peaceably when you try to take them captive?

252. There are no shortcuts to anywhere worth going.

253. Sometimes the pieces of your brokenness is what God uses to help others.

254. Men try to fix things with duct tape; Christ used nails.

255. You can't go back to yesterday, you are not that person anymore.

256. Some people find a cloud in every silver lining.

257. Don't build a road around a mountain that God called you to remove.

258. It feels good to be lost in the right direction.

259. Don't let emotions overpower your intelligence.

260. Don't find fault, find a remedy.

261. Words are free, it's how you use them that will cost you.

262. Life is short, use your important words.

263. The devil continues to make plays on the board, but he can't change the outcome of the game.

264. Never settle for staying where you are.

265. Define your vision & let nothing stop it.

266. You always have a choice.

267. It's hard to get the train back on the tracks when it's been derailed & twisted & the tracks have shifted.

268. About the time you decide to give up & go back is right when you should have gone a little further, but you didn't realize you were almost there.

269. Respect lasts longer than attention.

270. One risk you should avoid is the risk of doing nothing.

271. Overcome you, then you can overcome them.

272. A bend in the road is not the end of the road, unless you fail to make the turn.

273. Don't follow the crowd, you will get lost in it.

274. Beware those who derail you, they won't stick around to see you healed.

275. Turn your wounds into wisdom.

276. If someone is drowning, you don't tell them to enjoy the water, you throw them a Lifesaver....Jesus.

277. Some wisdom comes through healed pain.

278. Broken crayons, still color.

279. Don't look at where you fell, but where you slipped.

280. I didn't fall for you..you tripped me.

281. It's not the load that breaks you, it's how you carry it.

282. Making mistakes is better than faking perfection.

283. It's not what you look at,,,it's what you see.

284. One detour doesn't cancel your destination.

285. Pain is temporary, victory is forever.

286. When you close a chapter of your life, be sure to leave all the pages behind.

287. The mind replays what the heart can't delete.

288. Sometimes others must show us what we can't see.

289. If your presence doesn't make an impact, your absence makes no difference.

290. Just because you've been there before, doesn't mean you should be there now.

291. Funny how day by day nothing changes, but when you look back everything has.

292. It's what you say to yourself that matters.

293. Overcoming what you thought you couldn't makes you stronger.

294. Build bridges instead of burning them.

295. Magnify strengths not weaknesses.

296. Doesn't matter how accurate you are if you are aiming at the wrong goal.

297. If you quit, it means you never wanted it.

298. Doing the same thing over & over in the exact same way won't solve your problem.

299. It feels good to stick your head in the sand, but you can't keep it there long.

300. Love is always a demonstration.

301. Push through it.

302. You will be surprised how far you can go passed the point you thought was the end.

303. There's no excuse for becoming darkness to try to distinguish it.

304. May your life preach louder than your lips.

305. Don't waste who you are.

306. Eyes are useless if the mind is blind.

307. Don't punish those in front of you for the mistakes made by those behind you.

308. If you don't know your own worth no one else will either.

309. When you get knocked down, fall up!

310. Inspect your own fruit.

311. It's the journey not the destination.

312. Surround yourself with people on the same mission as you.

313. Be different to stand out.

314. Our lives are defined by opportunities even missed ones.

315. Walk away from anything that doesn't grow you.

316. When things don't add up in life, start subtracting.

317. If you live for people's acceptance, you will die by their rejection.

318. It's not all about you.

319. Actions speak louder than words, not just as often.

320. Truth is not diminished by the number of people who believe it.

321. Have cognition before ignition.

322. The One standing next to you is stronger than the one standing against you.

323. Give out what you want back.

324. Live well ..love better.

325. If all I see is my struggle, I can't see my freedom.

326. Joy is portable, take it with you.

327. Everyone dies, not everyone lives.

328. It's not about what you gather but what you scatter.

329. Grace finds you where you are, but doesn't leave you there.

330. Don't focus so hard in front of you that you don't enjoy where you are.

331. It's not about getting noticed, it's about being remembered.

332. When the chess game is over, the King & the Pawn go back in the same box.

333. Better to be slapped by truth than kissed with a lie.

334. Life might not be the party you hoped for but dance anyway.

335. The price of not having courage is great.

336. When you choose hope, anything is possible.

337. Two things run deep,,,love & heartache.

338. Christ didn't bring you out of that storm to die in this puddle.

339. Don't run back to what broke you.

340. Learn to say no without explanation.

341. One of the hardest things in life is to let go of what you thought was real.

342. Stars can't shine without darkness.

343. You are what you do, not what you say you will do.

344. A negative mind will never lead to a positive life.

345. Confusion comes when we try to convince our head of something our heart knows is a lie.

346. A good laugh & a long sleep will cure just about anything.

347. Confidence is silent, insecurity is loud.

348. Small deeds done are better than great deeds planned.

349. You can't walk the exact step twice.

350. When the moment is gone...it's gone.

351. Don't travel a dead end road.

352. If you learned something then the time was not wasted.

353. Moving fast is not the same as going somewhere.

354. Just because something has a price doesn't mean it has value.

355. The problem is not the problem, your attitude about the problem is the problem.

356. Don't make decisions today that will backfire on you tomorrow.

357. Sometimes to pick something up, you must put something down.

358. P.U.S.H. = pray until something happens.

359. What worries you, masters you.

360. Go in the direction of your dreams.

361. Once you accept your flaws no one can use them against you.

362. If you live on the edge, there will always be someone there to push you over.

363. Everyone you will meet knows something you don't.

364. If you figured it all out today, there would be no point in tomorrow.

365. Great things acquire time.

Made in the USA
Columbia, SC
11 August 2019